THE MEGA WOULD YOU RATHER? SIX-SEVEN GAME BOOK FOR KIDS

RIDDLELAND

TABLE OF CONTENTS

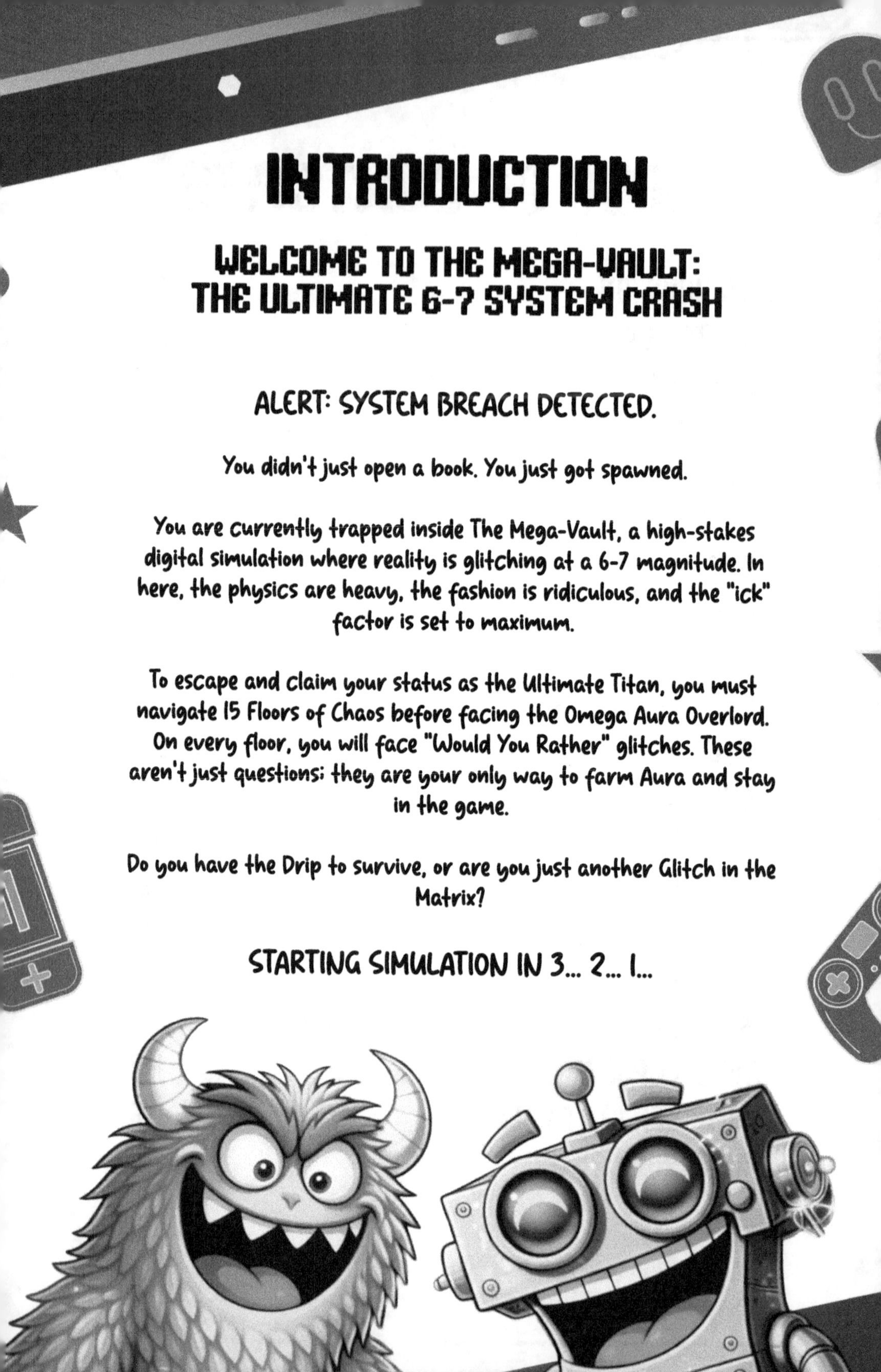

INTRODUCTION

WELCOME TO THE MEGA-VAULT: THE ULTIMATE 6-7 SYSTEM CRASH

ALERT: SYSTEM BREACH DETECTED.

You didn't just open a book. You just got spawned.

You are currently trapped inside The Mega-Vault, a high-stakes digital simulation where reality is glitching at a 6-7 magnitude. In here, the physics are heavy, the fashion is ridiculous, and the "ick" factor is set to maximum.

To escape and claim your status as the Ultimate Titan, you must navigate 15 Floors of Chaos before facing the Omega Aura Overlord. On every floor, you will face "Would You Rather" glitches. These aren't just questions: they are your only way to farm Aura and stay in the game.

Do you have the Drip to survive, or are you just another Glitch in the Matrix?

STARTING SIMULATION IN 3... 2... 1...

HOW TO PLAY:

THE MEGA-VAULT RULES

Yo! Welcome to the 6-7 Mega-Vault. You aren't just reading a book; you've just been spawned into a high-stakes digital simulation. To get out, you have to climb 15 Floors of Chaos and face the Omega Aura Overlord.

But watch out; the game is glitching. We've set the difficulty to "6-7" (That's Gen Z for Massive, Heavy, and Totally Over-the-Top). If you want to finish with Infinite Aura, you need to follow the rules.
This book is filled with Would You Rather...questions, all with a 6-7 Gen Z twist.

Here's how it works:

1. Read the question out loud.
Each one gives you two wild, weird, or downright ridiculous choices.

2. Pick the one you'd rather do.
Would you rather have a "Glow Up" that gains you 7 million fake followers OR a "Skill Up" that makes you the undisputed best gamer on Earth? It's up to you!

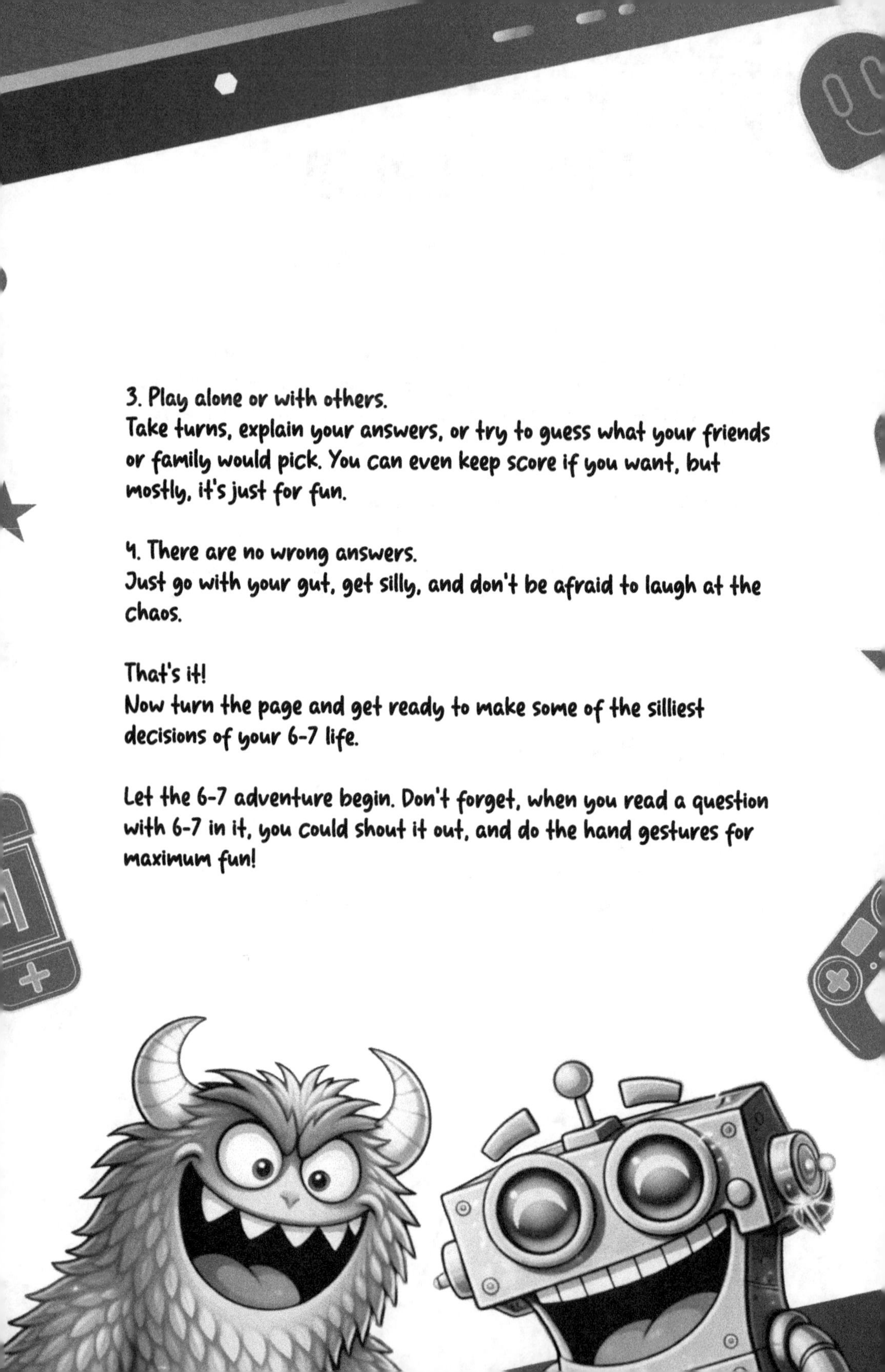

3. Play alone or with others.
Take turns, explain your answers, or try to guess what your friends or family would pick. You can even keep score if you want, but mostly, it's just for fun.

4. There are no wrong answers.
Just go with your gut, get silly, and don't be afraid to laugh at the chaos.

That's it!
Now turn the page and get ready to make some of the silliest decisions of your 6-7 life.

Let the 6-7 adventure begin. Don't forget, when you read a question with 6-7 in it, you could shout it out, and do the hand gestures for maximum fun!

(THE CHEAT SHEET):

Aura: Your vibe. More Aura = More Respect.

NPC: A "Non-Player Character." Someone who is boring and follows the crowd. (Avoid this!)

Drip: Your style/outfit.

Sigma: The top-tier leader: someone with Max Aura.

No Cap: "I'm not lying" / "For real."

Ratio: When someone gets more likes/points than you (usually because you said something cringe).

THE LOADING BAR IS AT 99%... THE SIMULATION IS STARTING...

ARE YOU READY TO CLIMB?

LEVEL 0

THE BRAINROT BASEMENT

You've descended into the Brainrot Basement.
This is where the physics of the simulation truly start to "glitch."
Magic here isn't just wands and hats; it's high-speed,
reality-warping chaos that can either skyrocket your Aura
or leave you looking like a total NPC.

THE "GLITCH-MAGIC" CHALLENGES

Would you rather turn invisible every time you sneeze

float 6-7 feet in the air every time you tell a lie?

Would you rather ride a pizza-shaped flying carpet

a broomstick powered by thousands of jellybeans?

Would you rather be best friends with a sarcastic dragon who calls you a "noob"

a genie who only grants 6 weird wishes a day?

Would you rather burp bubbles that pop with "cool" sounds

hiccup tiny frogs wearing top hats?

Would you rather have rainbow hair that changes with your mood,

eyebrows that shoot 7 pounds of glitter when you're surprised?

Would you rather wear shoes that sing opera every time you run,

a cape that giggles at 6 different volumes when someone compliments your drip?

Would you rather have a backpack that shoots confetti

a lunchbox that tells 7 knock-knock jokes before it lets you eat?

Would you rather freeze time to eat all your favorite snacks

rewind time 6-7 minutes to undo an embarrassing "cringe" moment?

Would you rather accidentally turn your homework into a stack of pancakes

turn your teacher into a sleepy unicorn with 6 different colors in its mane?

Would you rather cast a spell
that makes everyone dance "The Griddy" uncontrollably,

OR sing opera
while doing math homework?

Would you rather sneeze out tiny flying spellbooks

yawn and make your room instantly clean? (Infinite Aura Cheat Code!)

Would you rather go to a magical school where every class is a surprise,

a school where a hundred lockers all tell your secrets at once?

Would you rather live in a floating castle made of clouds

a treehouse that has talking elevators?

Would you rather have magical hiccups that change your outfit randomly,

magical yawns that turn off every light within 6-7 miles?

Would you rather have a wand that tells terrible dad jokes

a spellbook that never stops humming different viral theme songs?

Would you rather drink a potion that gives you a bouncy tail

one that makes your ears grow 6 inches every time you "cap" (lie or exaggerate)?

Would you rather be a wizard who only knows "glitch" spells

a fairy who sneezes clouds of glitter?

Would you rather accidentally summon a herd of 7 breakdancing goats

a cloud of singing marshmallows?

Would you rather ride a unicorn-chicken hybrid

a ten-ton dragon that is afraid of loud noises?

Would you rather sleep on a cloud that snores

a bed that floats and spins 7 times per minute all night?

Would you rather sneeze jellybeans

blink and accidentally turn your shoes into slices of toast?

Would you rather invent your own spell that only works on Tuesdays,

discover a new magical creature that can only whisper 6 secrets?

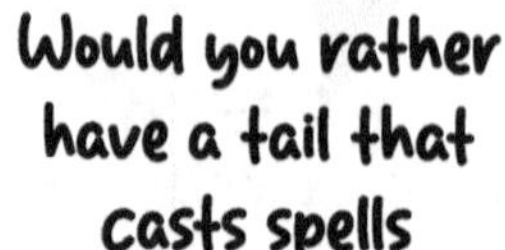

Would you rather have a tail that casts spells

a hat that floats 6-7 inches above your head and whispers advice?

Would you rather wear socks that glow like fireflies

mittens that clap 6 times every time you're happy?

Would you rather teleport into random storybooks

control the weather, but only inside a 7-foot circle around your bathroom?

Would you rather take flying lessons from a nervous broomstick

spell lessons from a sleepy owl that naps for hours mid-sentence?

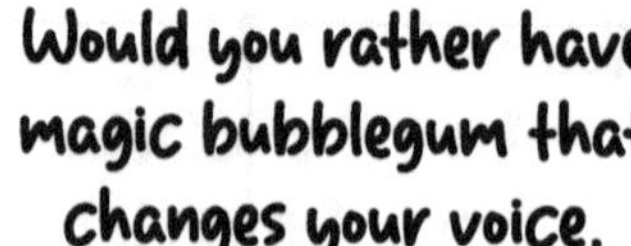

Would you rather have magic bubblegum that changes your voice,

enchanted sunglasses that show different brain-rot memes instead of reality?

Would you rather
be stuck in a magical board game

OR trapped in a potion lab filled
with thousands of riddles?

Would you rather
have a pocket dragon
that hiccups fire

a hamster that
accidentally casts "Bad
Luck" spells on NPCs?

Would you rather
switch places for a day
with a wizard-worm

a shape-shifting sandwich
that changes into 6
different flavors?

LEVEL COMPLETE?
YOU'VE SURVIVED THE MAGIC GLITCH!
Your Aura is currently peaking.

LEVEL 1
THE FOYER OF FRAGMENTATION

Welcome to the Foyer of Fragmentation. This is the outermost shell of the Mega Vault, but the server is struggling. The frame rate is tanking, the physics are cooked, and everyone around you is acting like a total NPC. If you want to begin your 14-floor climb to the Omega Aura Overlord, you have to survive the "Initial Glitch."

To breach the Vault, you must prove you have the Main Character Energy to handle a reality that is stuttering while your brain is at full throttle!

THE "FRAGMENTED FOYER" CHALLENGES

Would you rather walk like your Internet is cutting out,

have your voice lag so it comes out 10 seconds after you speak?

Would you rather have a "Loading Icon" spinning over your head all day,

have to T-Pose for 7 minutes whenever you meet a crush?

Would you rather be stuck in a "Conversation Loop" with a boring NPC

have your clothes reset to a "Default Skin" every 6 steps?

Would you rather only be able to move in "Grid Mode" (90-degree turns only)

jump 7 feet in the air every time you try to sit down?

Would you rather have a backpack that weighs 6 tons but looks empty,

OR a tiny wallet that is impossible to pick up?

Would you rather have your life narrated by a "Low-Quality" TikTok AI voice

have 6 different subtitles appear in front of your face every time you sneeze?

Would you rather wait in a 7-hour line for a snack,

eat a "Glitchy" burger that tastes like cold pixels?

Would you rather have "Rubber-Band" physics (every time you run, you snap back 6 feet)

walk through walls but get stuck halfway?

Would you rather always look like a "Low-Resolution" 144p photo,

have 7 identical clones of yourself following you and copying your every move?

Would you rather have your hair stay perfectly still like plastic,

have it flow in 6 different directions at once?

Would you rather only be able to speak in "Pre-set Dialogue Options"

have to do a "Fortnite Emote" for 6 minutes to unlock your front door?

Would you rather have a pet dog that teleports randomly every 7 seconds,

a cat that is 6 times bigger than a car?

Would you rather have your bedroom furniture float inches off the floor,

have your bed make "Error" sounds when you try to sleep?

Would you rather have a "Health Bar" over your head that drops when you're bored,

a "Stamina Bar" that runs out after 6 steps?

Would you rather wear shoes that make a "Windows Startup" sound every time you step,

a hat that plays loud, distorted elevator music?

Would you rather have to wait 7 minutes for your food to "Render" on your plate,

eat invisible food that tastes like 10/10 tacos?

Would you rather be stuck in a room with 6 mirrors that show you as an old man,

mirrors that show you as a baby?

Would you rather have your hands turn into "Lego Hands" for 6 hours,

have feet that are 7 times wider than your shoes?

Would you rather be "Mewing" for 7 days straight without talking,

lose -6,700 Aura by crying in public over a lost pen?

Would you rather have a "Ping" of 999 (everything you do happens way later)

have your vision "Buffer" every time you blink?

Would you rather have to wear a "Beta Tester" t-shirt forever

have a 7-foot neon arrow pointing at you that says "MAIN CHARACTER"?

Would you rather find 6 glitches in your breakfast (floating cereal)

have your school bus drive at 7 mph for the whole trip?

Would you rather have your shoes "Clip" through the floor so you're always ankle-deep,

OR have to wear 6 pairs of sunglasses at once?

Would you rather be the "Main Character" but everyone ignores you,

be an "NPC," but everyone thinks you're a legend?

Would you rather have your skin turn neon blue every time you're "Lagging"

grow 7 extra fingers that don't do anything?

Would you rather only be able to hear "8-bit" chiptune music

only see the world in "Night Vision" mode?

Would you rather have a "7/10" Aura rating but no friends,

a "0" Aura rating but you're the leader of a giant squad?

Would you rather have your internal clock run 6 minutes fast

7 minutes slow?

Would you rather trip over a "Hidden Hitbox" every time you run,

have to walk like a character from a 1920s cartoon?

Would you rather escape the Foyer but lose all your "Rare Skins"

stay in the entrance as the "King of Lag"?

LEVEL COMPLETE?
YOU'VE MADE IT THROUGH THE FRAGMENTATION!
Your connection to the Mega-Vault is stabilizing.
You've earned +1,000 Starting Aura.

LEVEL 2

THE AURA FARM

Welcome to The Aura Farm. On this floor, social credit is the only currency that matters. You aren't just surviving; you're trying to maximize your "Drip" (cool, stylish or trendy look) and avoid the dreaded "Negative Aura" abyss.

In the Farm, everything you do is being broadcast to the Mega Vault's internal feed. One wrong move and you're "cooked" (finished/defeated). One right move and you're a "Certified Legend" (cool, admirable).

THE "AURA FARMING" CHALLENGES

Would you rather have +1 Million Aura but you have to wear an "I'm an NPC" shirt forever,

have 0 Aura, but everyone treats you like the Final Boss?

Would you rather lose all your Aura by falling into a pool of baked beans

gain a 7,000-point Aura boost by successfully "Mewing" for an entire year?

Would you rather have a "Locked" Aura rating that never changes,

an Aura rating that resets to zero every time you sneeze?

Would you rather be caught "Aura Farming" in a crowded grocery store

be caught "Default Dancing" in detention?

Would you rather have a 6-foot neon sign above your head showing your "Cringe Level"

a tiny sign that only your crush can see?

Would you rather gain +1,000 Aura every time you say "No Cap"

lose Aura points every time you blink?

Would you rather have "Infinite Aura" but you look like a literal potato,

look like a supermodel but have -6.7 Million Aura?

Would you rather accidentally lose Aura by tripping on a flat surface,

lose your entire "Streak" by calling your teacher "Mom"?

Would you rather be the "Aura Leader" of 6 or 7 toddlers

be the lowest-ranking member of a Mega-Titan squad?

Would you rather your Aura
glow 7 different colors based on your mood,

OR have it stay "Solid Gold"
but only when you're asleep?

Would you rather
save a kitten for
+500 Aura

land a "God-Tier"
backflip for
+6,700 Aura?

Would you rather
your Aura smell
like "New Car"

have it smell
like 6-day-old tacos
but look visually stunning?

Would you rather lose your Aura Streak because you dropped your phone,

because you accidentally "liked" a post from 2019 on your enemy's profile?

Would you rather "Flex" your Aura to scare off a bully

use it to become the undisputed King of the 7th Grade?

Would you rather have a pet dog with 7 times more Aura than you,

a pet rock with "Infinite Aura"?

Would you rather your Aura be visible only in the dark,

only when you are doing something 6 times harder than normal?

Would you rather "Aura Farm" by helping old ladies cross the street,

by winning 6 Olympic Gold Medals in a single day?

Would you rather have a voice that sounds like different celebrities mixed together,

a face that turns into a "Crying Jordan" meme whenever you're embarrassed?

Would you rather have to "Pay" 7 Aura points every time you want a slice of pizza,

get free pizza that tastes like "Low-Aura" cardboard?

Would you rather be the Main Character of a movie with only 7 viewers

a background NPC in a movie with 7 billion viewers?

Would you rather have a backpack that generates 6 Aura points an hour,

shoes that make you run 7x faster but look like "Grandpa's Slippers"?

Would you rather your Aura be so heavy it cracks the floor,

so light that you float 6-7 inches off the ground?

Would you rather trade 7% of your total Aura for a lifetime supply of Takis

trade all your snacks for "God-Tier Aura"?

Would you rather "Glitch" your Aura so it looks like 1,000,000 to others,

have a Hidden Aura that only the "Omega Overlord" can detect?

Would you rather spend 6-7 hours in the "Cringe Zone" to double your points,

stay safe and gain nothing?

Would you rather be famous for a 7-second viral clip of you failing,

stay unknown while doing something legendary?

Would you rather your Aura be linked to your phone battery (1% = 0 Aura)

linked to your 7 closest friends' opinions of you?

Would you rather "Farm" Aura
by dancing in the rain

OR by solving math problems
without a calculator?

Would you rather have a 7-star rating on your Aura Card

a "Certified Legend" sticker that can never be removed?

Would you rather be the Boss of the Aura Farm

the owner of a building made entirely of Aura Crystals?

LEVEL COMPLETE?
YOU'VE SUCCESSFULLY HARVESTED ENOUGH AURA TO KEEP YOUR "SIGMA" STATUS. YOU ARE NO LONGER A "FOYER NOOB."
Prepare yourself...
the next floor of the Mega Vault
is loading.

LEVEL 3

THE HEAVY SNACK SHACK

Welcome to the Heavy Snack Shack, the most unhinged floor of the Mega-Vault. On this level, the physics of food have been sabotaged. Everything here is either massive, high-key disgusting, or carries a heavy risk of losing your Aura in front of the entire school.

If you make a "cringe" food choice here, you'll be stuck with Permanent NPC Energy for the rest of the game. Choose wisely to keep your hunger down and your Aura up!

THE "SNACK SHACK" CHALLENGES

Would you rather eat a 7-foot bowl of spaghetti using only your elbows while your crush watches,

finish a bowl of lukewarm jelly using only your eyebrows?

Would you rather have cotton candy hair that melts and gets sticky the second you get nervous,

have eyebrows made of crunchy pretzels that snap off whenever you're surprised?

Would you rather wear a taco hat that drips greasy salsa on your sneakers,

wear 7-pound peanut butter boots that leave "skid marks" on every floor?

Would you rather only be allowed to eat "aesthetic" purple foods,

only eat food that makes a crunch so loud it hits 70 decibels and interrupts the whole class?

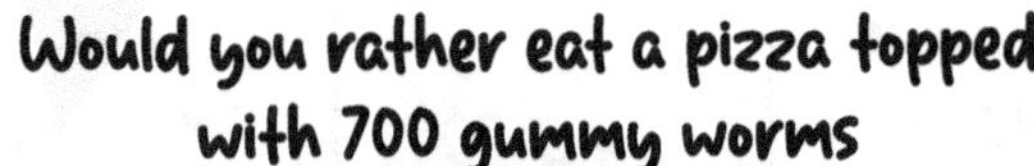

Would you rather eat a pizza topped with 700 gummy worms

OR a bowl of ice cream mixed with frozen hot dog chunks?

Would you rather sneeze ketchup for a week straight during flu season

cry maple syrup every time you see a "corecore" TikTok?

Would you rather take a bath in a pool of chocolate pudding in the middle of the mall,

have to swim through 7 tons of mashed potatoes while wearing a neon banana suit?

Would you rather eat a sandwich made of pickles and whipped cream

drink a smoothie made from 7 days of "mystery meat" school lunches?

Would you rather eat every dinner while bouncing on a trampoline

while riding a merry-go-round that spins 6 times faster than the legal limit?

Would you rather only eat breakfast for every meal

only eat desserts forever, but lose -5,000 Aura every time you smile?

Would you rather have a nose shaped like a 7-inch pickle

ears that look like floppy, buttered pancakes?

Would you rather be followed by a sentient hamburger that raps about your insecurities,

a donut that does a full ballet routine every 7 steps you take?

Would you rather
burp the national anthem
every time you eat
something sweet

hiccup 6 times in
a row every time you
try to act cool?

Would you rather
eat pancakes with
mint toothpaste syrup

eat a heaped plate
of raw broccoli dipped
in lukewarm
melted chocolate?

Would you rather
only eat food that
wobbles like Jell-O

food that is
as hard as a brick?

Would you rather
have pizza sauce flowing
through your veins

have 32 jellybeans
instead of teeth?

Would you rather
live in a house made
of toast that collapses
if you sneeze,

a cheese castle
that melts in 7 minutes if
the vibes get too "heated"?

Would you rather have whipped cream shoot from your fingers whenever you point at someone,

have a spray of canned cheese blast out whenever you try to dap someone up (greet them with a multi-step handshake)?

Would you rather have to yell "WOWSERS!" after every bite of food

whisper "scrumptious" in a Victorian accent?

Would you rather get hit in the face with a soggy pie every morning at 7:00 AM,

wake up inside a giant bowl of soggy cereal once per month?

Would you rather have chocolate chip freckles that melt into a mess when you're outside,

whipped cream hair that attracts a swarm of 7,000 bees?

Would you rather talk like a 1920s radio announcer every time you eat pizza,

sing opera while eating cake in front of 700 people you know?

Would you rather everything you eat
be spicy enough to ruin your day,

OR every drink you take be sour enough
to give you "lemon face" permanently?

Would you rather eat a cookie that screams "HELP!" when you bite it

a burrito that tells 7 "dad jokes" while you're trying to have a serious conversation?

Would you rather find a live worm in your sandwich

a raisin in your toothpaste?

Would you rather grow a random vegetable on your nose every Monday

shoot hot popcorn from your ears every time you get "pressed" (stressed)?

Would you rather only eat food that explodes into a cloud of glitter

food that makes your voice 7 times squeakier for an hour?

Would you rather be stuck in a cafeteria food fight against 7,000 meatballs

slip on a banana peel in front of the person you have a crush on?

Would you rather have a pet pizza that growls when you try to eat it,

a pet banana that sings depressing lullabies when it's "sleepy"?

Would you rather make your own lunch while blindfolded every morning,

have your lunch made by a clumsy raccoon with butter-fingers?

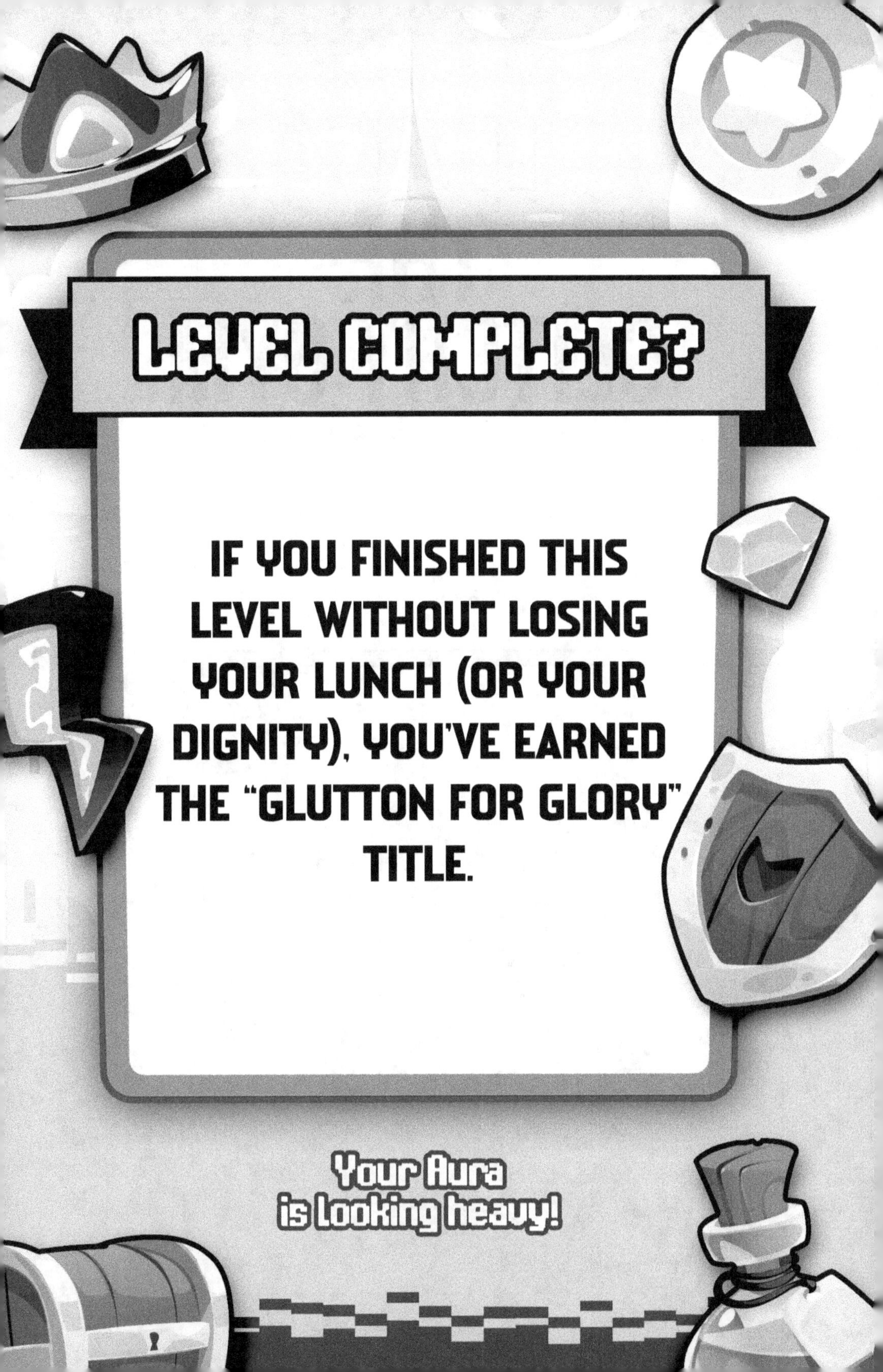

LEVEL COMPLETE?

IF YOU FINISHED THIS LEVEL WITHOUT LOSING YOUR LUNCH (OR YOUR DIGNITY), YOU'VE EARNED THE "GLUTTON FOR GLORY" TITLE.

Your Aura
is looking heavy!

LEVEL 4

THE GLITCHY GYM

You've reached the Glitchy Gym, where the physics engine is officially broken. This floor is all about Main Character Energy, but the powers you're getting are... well, a bit "glitchy." If you want to farm Infinite Aura, you have to master these bizarre abilities without looking like a total NPC.

THE "GLITCHY POWER" CHALLENGES

Would you rather fly, but only while sneezing six or seven times in a row,

become invisible, but only when no one is looking?

Would you rather have laser eyes that only work when you're terrified

super strength that only kicks in after exactly 6.7 hours of sleep?

Would you rather teleport, but always land upside down,

run at super speed while stuck in a permanent backward moonwalk?

Would you rather read minds, but the thoughts are all in Pig Latin,

talk to animals, but they give you sarcastic insults?

Would you rather grow a second head that gives you "low-aura" advice,

an extra hand that won't stop waving at every stranger you pass?

Would you rather glow like a neon lava lamp when trying to be stealthy,

shoot spaghetti from your sleeves when you're nervous?

Would you rather shrink to the size of a bug for a few seconds,

grow giant, but only your feet reach huge proportions?

Would you rather talk to machines, but they all complain about "lag,"

breathe underwater, but only in a kiddie pool that is 6-7 inches deep?

Would you rather float like a balloon when you're hyped

stick to walls like a magnet every time you're embarrassed?

Would you rather burp
6-7 bolts of actual lightning

OR sneeze a massive,
blinding cloud of glitter?

Would you rather
teleport into random
"glitch" locations
like a petting zoo

turn invisible,
but your "drip" (clothes)
stays visible?

Would you rather
wear a cape that never
stops flapping in your face

boots that shout "POW!"
at seven different volumes
with every step?

Would you rather make it snow inside your living room

fly just high enough to bump into every single ceiling fan?

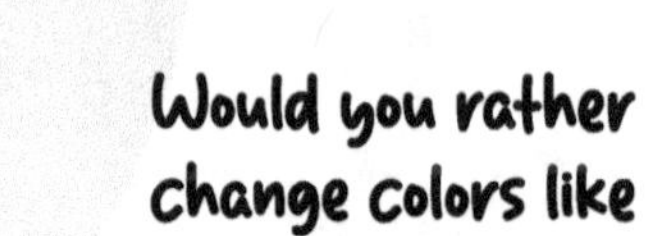

Would you rather change colors like a chameleon based on your mood,

glow bright green whenever someone within 6 feet of you tells a lie (The No-Cap Detector)?

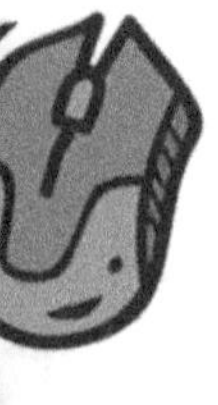

Would you rather have X-ray vision that only works on fruit,

super hearing that only picks up people whispering secrets about you?

Would you rather grow wings that flap every time you blink,

a tail that wags uncontrollably for 7 minutes whenever you see your crush?

Would you rather freeze time for a few seconds

rewind time just enough to avoid a "Mega-Cringe" moment?

Would you rather turn into a liquid puddle to escape danger,

shoot jelly from your ears when startled by a loud noise?

Would you rather wear a superhero suit that smells like 7-day-old gym socks

a cape that tickles your neck constantly?

Would you rather shoot glitter from your eyes

emit a trail of bubbles from your feet every time you run?

Would you rather have mind control, but only over a squad of pigeons,

super speed, but only while spinning in circles?

Would you rather stretch like a rubber band but bounce uncontrollably,

move 7 times slower than a background NPC?

Would you rather have a secret identity that everyone already knows,

a sidekick who is terrified of 7 different types of cheese?

Would you rather have to tell every joke in slow motion

skip every class where the teacher mentions "Homework"?

Would you rather turn into a cloud when you're bored

melt into 6-7 gallons of blue Gatorade when you're tired?

Would you rather have hiccups that physically rearrange your furniture

sneezes that instantly change your outfit style?

Would you rather fly like a pro but only while wearing clown shoes,

OR

turn invisible, but only while holding your breath for 6 seconds?

Would you rather talk to plants,
but they gossip about your search history,

OR control fire,
but only enough to toast a few marshmallows?

Would you rather
wear a belt that loudly
announces your "Aura Level"

gloves that clap
every time you finish
a sentence?

Would you rather
invent your own ridiculous
"Glitch" power

trade abilities with
a hamster that has 6-7
million followers on TikTok?

LEVEL COMPLETE?
YOU'VE MASTERED THE GLITCHY GYM!
Your power level
is officially OVER 9000
(and your Aura is looking massive).

LEVEL 5

THE "NO-CAP" NATURE ZONE

You've entered the No-Cap Nature Zone. This isn't your average petting zoo. The physics are warped, the animals have "main character energy," and if you don't choose the high-aura path, you're just an NPC in a world of Titans.

THE "NO-CAP" CREATURE CHALLENGES

Would you rather have a monkey tail

rabbit ears that pick up 5G signals?

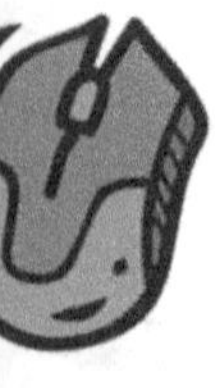

Would you rather sleep upside down like a bat (Major Aura)

in a shell like a turtle?

Would you rather roar like a lion

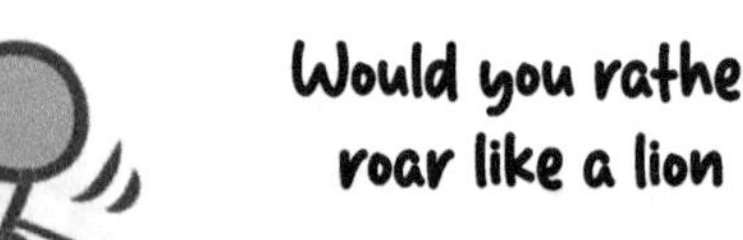

howl like a wolf every time you catch a Victory Royale?

Would you rather hop like a kangaroo

slither like a snake while Aura farming through the mall?

Would you rather
have a pet dinosaur

OR a pet unicorn
that eats your homework every morning?

Would you rather
do backflips
like a dolphin

balance like a flamingo
on one leg for
6 hours straight?

Would you rather
shed your skin
like a snake

grow a fresh
set of feathers
every single week?

Would you rather talk to animals, but they all call you a "Chatterbox NPC,"

only talk to bugs who treat you like a king?

Would you rather live in a treehouse with a squad of monkeys

underwater with dolphins who only speak in glitch-core beats?

Would you rather ride a flying eagle with a 6-7 meter wingspan

a cheetah equipped with a Turbo engine?

Would you rather purr like a cat when you're vibing

bark like a dog whenever your WiFi lags?

Would you rather eat like a panda (bamboo)

only eat raw fish like a shark?

Would you rather
be as small as an ant
(0.001 Aura)

as big as
a 6-7 story giraffe?

Would you rather
race a snail
on a skateboard

a turtle
on roller skates?

Would you rather
be a flying octopus

a swimming
giraffe?

Would you rather
get chased by a stampede
of 600 squirrels

one single flock
of very angry chickens?

Would you rather
nap in a fox den

have a squad of
monkeys braid your hair
while you sleep?

Would you rather brush your teeth with a porcupine quill

bathe in a tiny birdbath?

Would you rather talk to dogs (but lose your human speech)

understand cats but stay silent to keep your Mewing streak?

Would you rather get a piggyback ride from a 6-ton gorilla

chill in a kangaroo's pouch?

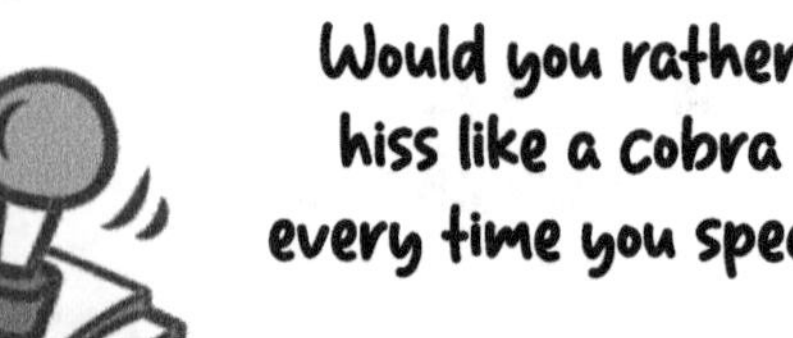

Would you rather hiss like a cobra every time you speak

chirp like a bird every time you blink?

Would you rather have a squirrel in your backpack who throws acorns at NPCs,

a raccoon in your closet with signature dance moves?

Would you rather have a staring contest with an owl

OR a dance battle with a flamingo?

Would you rather sleep in a giant bird nest

burrow underground like a mole for 6-7 days?

Would you rather wear a penguin tuxedo all year (Formal Drip)

an itchy woolly sheep coat?

Would you rather live one full day as your favorite animal

switch animal bodies every 6 minutes?

Would you rather spray a skunk smell when you're scared,

bray like a donkey when you're flexing?

Would you rather have a nose like an elephant

a neck that is 7 feet long?

Would you rather be raised by wolves

be taught Aura and manners by a council of parrots?

Would you rather sneeze out a cloud of feathers

hiccup the sound of a screaming goat?

LEVEL COMPLETE?

IF YOU MADE IT THROUGH THE ZOO WITHOUT LOSING YOUR COOL, YOU'VE OFFICIALLY UNLOCKED THE "BEAST MODE" BADGE.

LEVEL 6
THE CRINGE CORRIDOR

Welcome to the Cringe Corridor. This isn't just about being gross; it's a high-stakes battle for your social standing. In this level, every "ick" drains your battery, and one wrong move sends your reputation into the abyss.

THE "AURA OR ICK" CHALLENGES

Would you rather eat a 6-foot sandwich stuffed with actual worms

drink a pickle-juice milkshake on a livestream with 10 million viewers?

Would you rather have spaghetti for hair that "glitches" whenever you move,

have marshmallows for teeth?

Would you rather always smell like stinky socks (-100 Aura)

always smell like sour milk?

Would you rather burp glitter every time you speak (High Aura!)

fart bubbles every time you walk?

Would you rather
step in dog poop
with bare feet

have a massive booger
on your elbow during your
first TV interview?

Would you rather
get gum stuck
in your hair

have 6 bottles of
superglue stuck to
your hands forever?

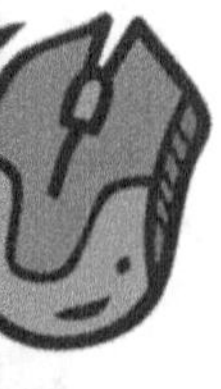

Would you rather
wear the same sweaty
gym shirt for a month

wear the same
crusty socks
for 7 weeks?

Would you rather
have green slime leak
from your ears

have a mountain of whipped
cream explode from your
nose every time you sneeze?

Would you rather
pick your nose in front
of the whole class,

accidentally spit on your
crush while explaining your
Aura farming strategy?

Would you rather lick a moldy slice of bread

OR bite into a raw onion like an apple while trying to keep a Mewing streak?

Would you rather always have sticky, "glitchy" fingers

always have a giant piece of broccoli stuck in your front teeth?

Would you rather eat a bug-flavored jellybean

drink a gallon jug of ketchup-flavored soda?

Would you rather have a permanent wedgie you can't fix,

wear itchy "NPC" underwear that never stops chafing?

Would you rather throw up rainbow slime every Friday

sneeze out a pound of spaghetti every time you giggle?

Would you rather brush your teeth with ketchup

wash your face with 6 scoops of mayonnaise?

Would you rather have a burping contest at a fancy wedding

a farting contest in a library where the silence makes it 7 times louder?

Would you rather have a tongue covered in hair

ears filled with a pound of wax?

Would you rather swim in a pool of chocolate syrup

a pool of cold, mashed potatoes that feels like a 7-ton weight?

Would you rather sit on a melting ice cream cone

step on a squishy pizza slice with 7 weird toppings?

Would you rather wear underwear on your head for a day,

wear 7 pairs of socks on your hands for a week?

Would you rather only be able to talk in burps

laugh like a goat every time you see a meme?

Would you rather eat cereal with orange juice

spaghetti covered in 7 layers of chocolate syrup?

Would you rather have armpits that smell like rotten eggs

feet that smell like a week-old dead fish?

Would you rather have a belly button that sprays whipped cream

ears that play circus music every hour?

Would you rather be covered in fluffy dog fur

have skin as slimy as a giant frog?

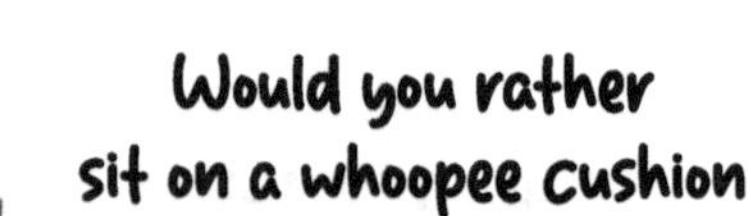

Would you rather sit on a whoopee cushion in the middle of a test

trip and land in a bowl of mashed potatoes that is 6 feet wide?

Would you rather eat a cupcake that tastes like broccoli

broccoli that tastes like a 7-layer chocolate cake?

Would you rather
get sneezed on by a 7-ton elephant

OR licked by a giant,
slimy lizard?

Would you rather
drool every time
you talk

hiccup every time
you blink?

Would you rather
sit in a massive
puddle of ketchup

get hit in the face
with a 6-pound
cream pie?

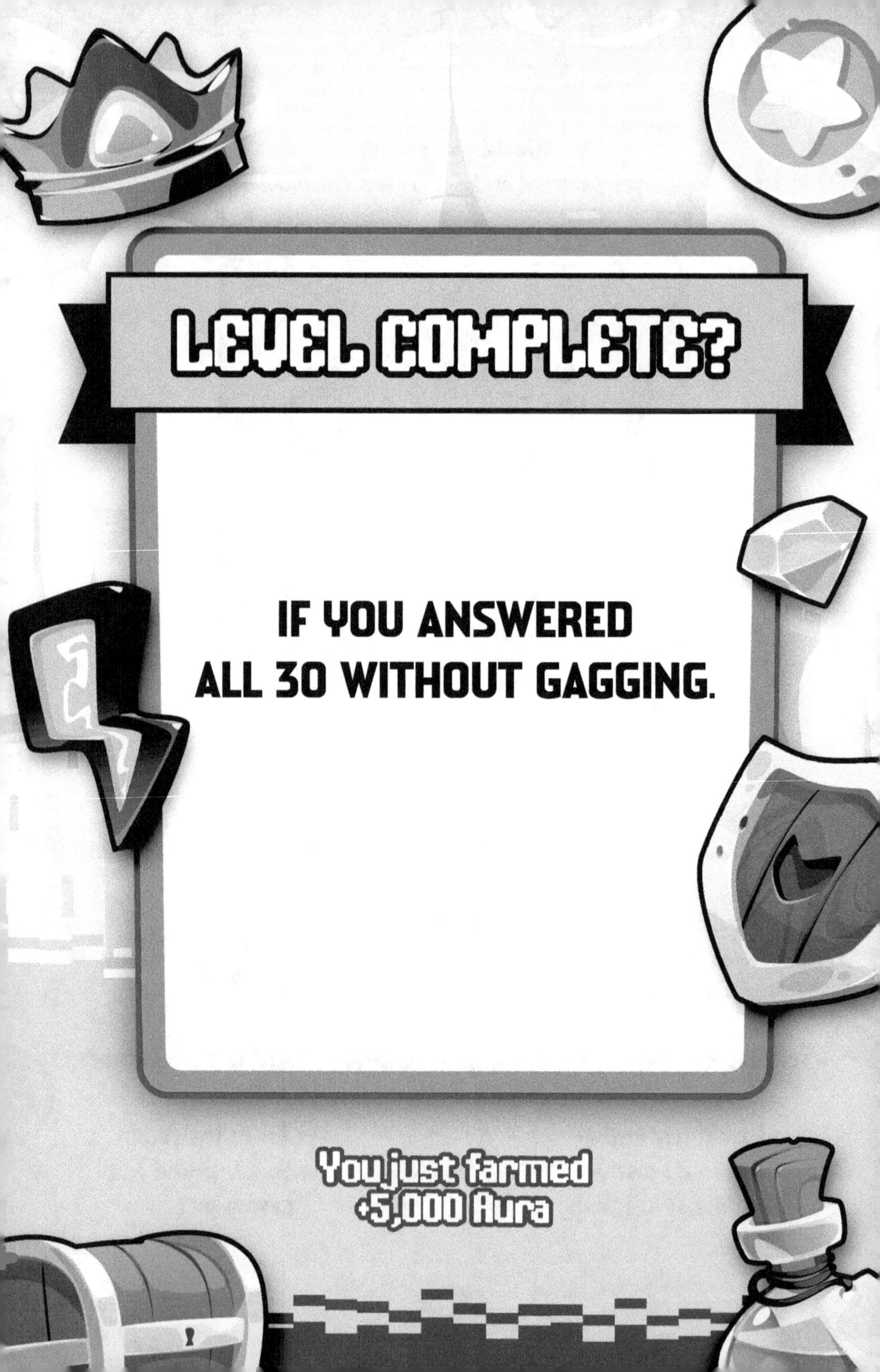
LEVEL COMPLETE?
IF YOU ANSWERED
ALL 30 WITHOUT GAGGING.
You just farmed
+5,000 Aura

LEVEL 7
THE POV PORTAL

You've just stepped through the POV Portal, and reality is starting to glitch. In this level, your perspective is completely cooked. You aren't just looking at the world; you're looking through shifting filters that change how reality renders. If you can't handle the visual lag, you'll lose your sense of direction and your Aura will drop to zero!

To beat this floor, you have to choose how you want to see, and be seen, in a world where the camera angle is everything.

THE "POV PORTAL" CHALLENGES

POV: You're a 6-7 Titan.
Would you rather have to duck under every single doorway

be the permanent captain of an undefeated pro basketball team?

POV: Third-Person View.
Would you rather control your body with a laggy controller

see a floating "Health Bar" above everyone's head?

POV: Silent Movie.
Would you rather have subtitles appear in the air every time you think,

have a loud, dramatic piano play whenever you walk into a room?

POV: The Main Character Streamer.
Would you rather have a "Live Chat" in your vision, giving you constant compliments,

one that calls you "Mid" (mediocre) every time you trip?

POV: The Micro-Ant.

Would you rather see blades of grass as skyscrapers

OR see a single raindrop as a 7-ton water bomb?

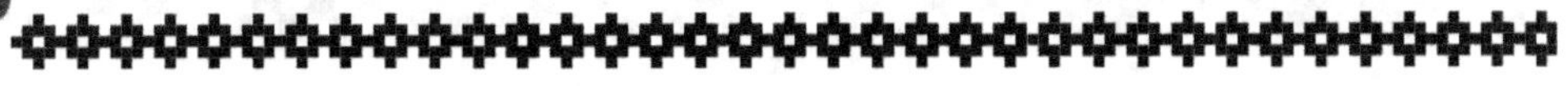

POV: Fish-Eye Lens.

Would you rather have everything look 6-7 times wider,

have your own nose look like a giant mountain in the middle of your vision?

POV: Thermal Vision.

Would you rather see everyone as glowing orange blobs

see your food as a block of frozen blue light?

POV: The Apex Predator.
Would you rather see the world from 7 miles up

have "Eagle Eye" vision that lets you see a crumb on the floor from the ceiling?

POV: The Glitch.
Would you rather see the world in neon colors that shouldn't exist,

see everyone's face replaced by their most-used emoji?

POV: Baby Vision.
Would you rather see your dog as a 6-ton barking monster

see your high chair as a giant, golden throne?

POV: Slow Motion.
Would you rather see a ball flying at you 7 times slower than normal,

hear everyone's voice slowed down into a deep, creepy growl?

POV: Fast Forward.
Would you rather finish a whole school day in 7 minutes

have your hair grow 7 inches every time you blink?

POV: The Mega-Giant.
Would you rather see clouds as fluffy pillows you can actually touch,

see the ocean as a small puddle you can jump over?

POV: Meme Filters.
Would you rather have everyone look like they have "Infinite Aura"

see the world rendered as a retro 8-bit video game?

POV: The House Cat.
Would you rather see humans as giant, 7-foot-tall can openers

see a laser pointer as the most important mission in the galaxy?

POV: Cringe-Vision.
Would you rather see a neon "CRINGE" sign flash over people when they tell bad jokes,

have a "W" appear over your head every time you do something cool?

POV: Night Vision.
Would you rather see everything in a glowing green tint

have your own eyes glow like high-beam flashlights in the dark?

POV: The Kaiju.
Would you rather have to wear school buses as shoes

use a neighborhood swimming pool as your cereal bowl?

POV: X-Ray Vision.
Would you rather see what's inside every "Mystery Box" before you buy it

see through 7 layers of wrapping paper on your birthday?

POV: The Gamer.
Would you rather have a "Mini-Map" in the corner of your eye

see "Achievement Unlocked" pop up every time you eat a snack?

POV: Gravity Glitch.
Would you rather walk on the ceiling for 7 hours,

have to eat your lunch while hanging upside down from your knees?

POV: Drip-Vision.
Would you rather see everyone's "Fit Rating" out of 100,

be able to change your own outfit instantly just by snapping your fingers?

POV: The Ghost.

Would you rather be able to see through walls

OR walk through 7 people a day without them feeling it?

POV: Mirror World.

Would you rather have to read everything backward

have your left and right hands switch jobs for an entire week?

POV: Time-Vision.

Would you rather see what happens 7 seconds into the future,

see what happened 7 years in the past?

POV: Cartoon-Vision.
Would you rather see "BOOM!" bubbles appear when you run,

have your heart pop out of your chest like a spring when you're surprised?

POV: Pixel-Vision.
Would you rather look like a 3D character in a 2D world,

look like a low-res pixel character in a 4K world?

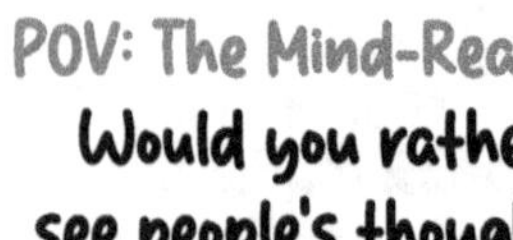

POV: The Mind-Reader.
Would you rather see people's thoughts as speech bubbles

see their "Aura Level" as a glowing number above their head?

POV: No-Cap Vision.
Would you rather see people's noses grow 7 inches when they lie,

see their pants actually catch on fire?

POV: The Final Boss.
Would you rather see the whole Mega-Vault from the top floor,

own the 7 most legendary POV filters in existence?

LEVEL COMPLETE?
YOUR VISION HAS STABILIZED, AND YOUR AURA IS LOOKING SHARP FROM EVERY ANGLE.
You've mastered the POV Portal!

LEVEL 8
THE STREAMER'S SURVIVAL GRID

Welcome to the Survival Grid. You aren't just playing the game anymore; you're being live-streamed to 6.7 billion viewers across the Mega-Vault. Your "Chat" is moving so fast the pixels are screaming, and your Aura is being voted on in real-time.

On this floor, you have to maintain peak "Main Character" energy while navigating lag, toxic trolls, and "Stream Snipers" trying to end your run. Don't go AFK (Away From Keyboard), or it's an instant Game Over.

THE "STREAMER SURVIVAL" CHALLENGES

Would you rather have a live "Face-Cam" hovering two inches from your nose all day,

a "Green Screen" stuck to your back that displays brain-rot memes to everyone behind you?

Would you rather have your "Live Chat" read out loud by a monotone robot voice every time you think,

have a "Donation Alert" scream at 100% volume every time you sneeze?

Would you rather have a squad of "Stream Snipers" follow you to school to steal your lunch,

experience a "Lag Spike" that freezes you in a cringe pose for 7 minutes during gym class?

Would you rather have to say "Thanks for the Sub!" to every person you make eye contact with,

do a forced victory dance every time you finish a sentence?

Would you rather have a "Sub Goal" bar on your forehead that says "7 subs until I wash my hair"

a "Follower Count" above your head that drops every time you say something "Cringe"?

Would you rather play every video game with a 7-second delay,

have your controller/mouse turn into a piece of slimy wet ham?

Would you rather be a "Viral Legend" for accidentally eating a giant bowl of mayo on camera,

be an "Unknown Pro" who is the best in the world but has zero followers?

Would you rather have your "Drip" rated by 6 million trolls

have your "Aura" judged by one very honest, 7-ton gorilla?

Would you rather have a "Life Battle Pass" that requires 7 backflips to unlock breakfast,

have all your snacks locked behind a literal paywall?

Would you rather have a "Bit Rate" so low you look like a blurry 8-bit block,

OR a "Ping" so high that you accidentally clip through walls?

Would you rather "Leak" your most embarrassing secret to 700 viewers

have your Search History displayed on a billboard in the school hallway?

Would you rather have a "Hype Train" follow you around playing ear-blasting music,

be stuck in "Emote Only" mode where you can only communicate with hand gestures?

Would you rather wear a 7-pound headset that you can't take off,

have a gaming chair that follows you and tries to aggressively sit you down every 5 minutes?

Would you rather get "Raided" by 6,000 friendly puppies

"Raided" by a squad of people dressed as giant, dancing bananas?

Would you rather have your life "Moderated" by your parents who "Ban" you for 7 minutes every time you use slang,

have no moderators and pure, unhinged chaos?

Would you rather have a "Face Filter" glitch that gives you 7 extra eyes

one that turns your head into a spinning taco?

Would you rather have a keyboard missing the "W" key (No Wins!)

a mouse that moves in the opposite direction for 7 hours a day?

Would you rather
lose Aura points every time
a viewer "Unsubscribes"

have to eat a "Mystery
Bean" for every new
follower you gain?

Would you rather
do a "24-Hour Stream"
of you just doing math
homework,

a 7-minute stream of you
fighting a world-class MMA
fighter in real life?

Would you rather
have your webcam stuck on
"Beauty Filter" (Max Aura)

"Ogre Filter"
(Negative Aura)
for a full week?

Would you rather
have "Stream Snipers" hide
your shoes every morning

change your phone's
ringtone to a 7-minute song
about farts that can't be
silenced?

Would you rather
have a "Sponsor"
that forces you to wear
7 layers of winter clothes
in the summer,

a sponsor that makes you
eat raw broccoli on
camera once an hour?

Would you rather have a "Voice Filter" that makes you sound like a literal toddler

one that makes you sound like a grumpy, distorted robot?

Would you rather be "Banned" from the Mega-Vault for a week,

play on "Hard Mode" where every single NPC (including your teachers) is a Final Boss?

Would you rather have a "Glow Up" that gains you 7 million fake followers

a "Skill Up" that makes you the undisputed best gamer on Earth?

Would you rather have a "Chat Bot" that shouts "No Cap!" every time you speak,

a bot that loudly counts how many times you blink?

Would you rather have a "VR Headset" stuck to your face showing a 7-story fantasy world,

a "Microphone" that live-records and broadcasts your dreams?

Would you rather have "Infinite Battery"
but zero WiFi,

OR "Infinite WiFi"
but your phone dies every 7 minutes?

Would you rather win a "Streamer Award" that weighs 7 tons and must be kept in your room,

a "Mystery Key" that opens any locked door in the Mega-Vault?

Would you rather be the "Top Streamer" of Level 8

the "Final Boss" of the entire Simulation?

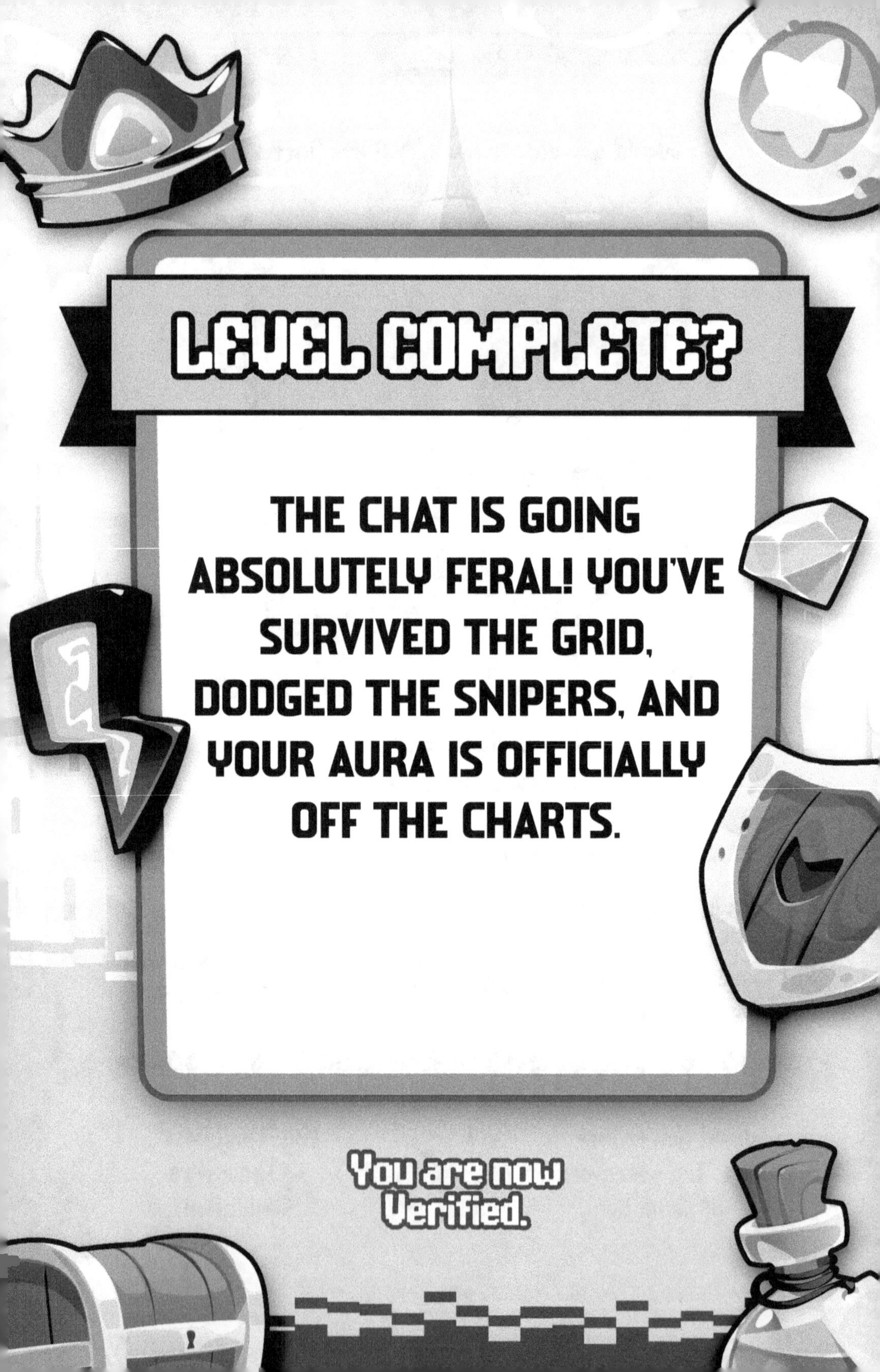
LEVEL COMPLETE?
THE CHAT IS GOING ABSOLUTELY FERAL! YOU'VE SURVIVED THE GRID, DODGED THE SNIPERS, AND YOUR AURA IS OFFICIALLY OFF THE CHARTS.
You are now Verified.

LEVEL 9
THE FASHION FAIL-SAFE

Welcome to Level 9, the "Drip Check" of the century. In the Mega-Vault, your outfit isn't just clothes; it's your power level. The "Fashion Fail-Safe" has been triggered, meaning the simulation is forcing you to rock the weirdest fits in the database.

Will you have the Drip to pull it off, or will you Drown in the cringe?

THE "DRIP OR DROWN" CHALLENGES

Would you rather wear 6 layers of puffer jackets in a heatwave

a swimsuit made of frozen waffles?

Would you rather wear sneakers that are 7 sizes too big

have to wear socks on your hands for a week?

Would you rather have "Drip" so hard it literally leaks water everywhere you walk,

a "Glow" so bright you look like a stadium floodlight?

Would you rather wear a cape that won't stop flapping in your face

a 6-foot-tall top hat that hits every ceiling fan?

Would you rather wear
a penguin tuxedo all year (High Aura!)

OR an itchy woolly sheep coat
that weighs 67 pounds?

Would you rather have "Infinite Drip," but you can only walk backward,

wear "NPC Default Skins," but move 6x faster than everyone else?

Would you rather wear a taco hat that drips salsa on your shirt,

peanut butter shoes that stick to the floor for 7 steps every time you move?

Would you rather have RGB hair that changes color with your mood

eyebrows that shoot glitter cannons whenever you're surprised?

Would you rather wear 7 pairs of sunglasses at once,

one pair of glasses that are 6 feet wide?

Would you rather have your fit rated "0/10" by a supermodel

"10/10" by a squad of stinky skunks?

Would you rather wear underwear on your head for a day,

6 layers of itchy sweaters in the Sahara Desert?

Would you rather have shoes that sing opera every time you run

boots that shout "POW!" with every single step?

Would you rather have a "Main Character" glowing outline

be invisible, but your chunky 7-ton sneakers stay visible?

Would you rather wear a belt that loudly announces your Aura Level,

gloves that do a forced clap every time you speak?

Would you rather have hair made of marshmallows

hair made of cooked spaghetti that never dries?

Would you rather wear a superhero suit that smells like old cheese

a cape that tickles you constantly?

Would you rather have "Drip," that changes color every time you blink,

be permanently stuck in a giant hot dog costume?

Would you rather
wear mittens that clap
whenever you're happy

socks that
glow like fireflies?

Would you rather
have your backpack
follow you like a puppy

have your clothes
"tattle" on you whenever
you try to sneak a snack?

Would you rather
wear a suit made of
candy wrappers

an outfit made entirely of
bubble wrap (and everyone
wants to pop you)?

Would you rather
have a 7-foot-long scarf
that trips everyone,

a tie that is
so short it's basically
a button?

Would you rather
have your "Drip" be
"No Cap" (it forces you
to be honest),

have your hat fly off
every time you tell a lie?

Would you rather
wear 7 watches on each arm

OR one giant clock around
your neck like a heavy anchor?

Would you rather
have sneakers that make
"Squeaky Toy" sounds

boots that make
"T. rex" stomping sounds?

Would you rather
have a hat that whispers
"Aura Farming" tips
in your ear,

a hoodie that
hugs you whenever
you're stressed?

Would you rather wear a wig made of neon wires

have eyebrows that grow 6 inches every time you sneeze?

Would you rather be "Best Dressed" in a zombie apocalypse

"Worst Dressed" at a celebrity red carpet?

Would you rather wear a necklace made of spicy peppers

a bracelet made of stinging nettles?

Would you rather have your shoes "glitch" through the floor,

have your pants be 7 feet too long so you're constantly stumbling?

Would you rather be the "Icon of Drip" for the whole Mega-Vault

have "Infinite Aura" while wearing a literal trash bag?

LEVEL COMPLETE?
YOU'VE SUCCESSFULLY BYPASSED THE FASHION FAIL-SAFE! YOUR FIT IS LOOKING HEAVY AND YOUR AURA IS PEAKED.
You're officially too cool for the simulation.

LEVEL 10

THE HOMEWORK HEIST

Welcome to Level 10. The school sim has been hacked! Your GPA doesn't matter here; only your Aura Score does. The classrooms are glitching, the teachers are NPCs with broken pathfinding, and the school supplies are acting way more unhinged than usual.

If you want to graduate to the next floor, you'll have to survive the most chaotic school day in the history of the Mega-Vault.

THE "6-7" SCHOOL SHENANIGANS

Would you rather take every test while bouncing on a pogo stick

wear squeaky clown shoes that honk with every single step?

Would you rather have a math teacher who only speaks in Pirate-core

a science teacher who hides 6-7 whoopee cushions around the room every lesson?

Would you rather have recess on the moon

gym class inside a bouncy castle the size of a skyscraper?

Would you rather forget your backpack every day

carry one so massive it drags behind you like a 6-ton parade float?

Would you rather turn into a giant pencil during Art

a singing dictionary that only defines brain-rot slang?

Would you rather sit next to a unicorn that won't stop farting glitter

a robot that explodes with confetti 6 times per hour?

Would you rather have a school bell that screams "TACOS!"

lockers that moo like a herd of cows every time they're opened?

Would you rather accidentally glue your hands to your desk

have permanent glitter stuck in your eyebrows for 6-7 months?

Would you rather be the only kid who can't stop hiccupping

the only one who laughs at everything?

Would you rather
get a gold star for every hiccup

OR win "Class Clown" points
for making goat noises during history class?

Would you rather
eat mystery meat that
literally growls at you,

only be allowed to drink
6-7 gallons of pudding
through a tiny straw?

Would you rather
whisper every answer in
a robot voice

yell every answer
like a pirate during
a high-stakes quiz?

Would you rather switch places with your teacher for a day,

have your teacher replaced by a pet turtle in a suit?

Would you rather do homework with onion-scented crayons

be forced to write a long essay using only emojis?

Would you rather take spelling tests with made-up words

do math problems where the numbers change while you're solving them?

Would you rather ride a llama to school

skateboard through the hallway wearing a glittery cape and 6 pairs of sunglasses at once?

Would you rather have a locker that tells embarrassing jokes about you,

a desk that wiggles every time you tell a lie?

Would you rather have your principal turn into a talking grilled cheese

your bus driver turn into a sleepy sloth who snores loudly?

Would you rather attend class while riding a rollercoaster

while floating in zero gravity for the entire day?

Would you rather take a pop quiz on how to speak "Dolphin"

write a 7-page deep-dive into what your left sock is thinking?

Would you rather serve detention with a marching band of 6 hundred ducks

read with a ghost who has a really aggressive British accent?

Would you rather wear pajamas to school every day

a superhero costume with a cape that flaps?

Would you rather have a backpack that tattles on you to the teacher

pencils that scream "WHEEEE!" every time you write?

Would you rather have a cafeteria that serves desserts the size of beach balls,

one where the food explodes into glitter?

Would you rather sit on a Jell-O chair that won't stop wobbling

use a ruler that sings opera every time you draw a line?

Would you rather get an "A+" every time you tell a joke

get a free snack every time you raise your hand?

Would you rather act out every story you read in full costume,

be forced to draw your math answers because numbers are "banned"?

Would you rather have your backpack follow you like a loyal puppy

OR have your notebook talk back to you for 6-7 minutes every morning?

Would you rather walk into the wrong classroom every single day

have your desk float in the air every time you take a test?

Would you rather have a magical eraser that deletes your mistakes

a pen that draws dancing dinosaurs whenever you're bored in class?

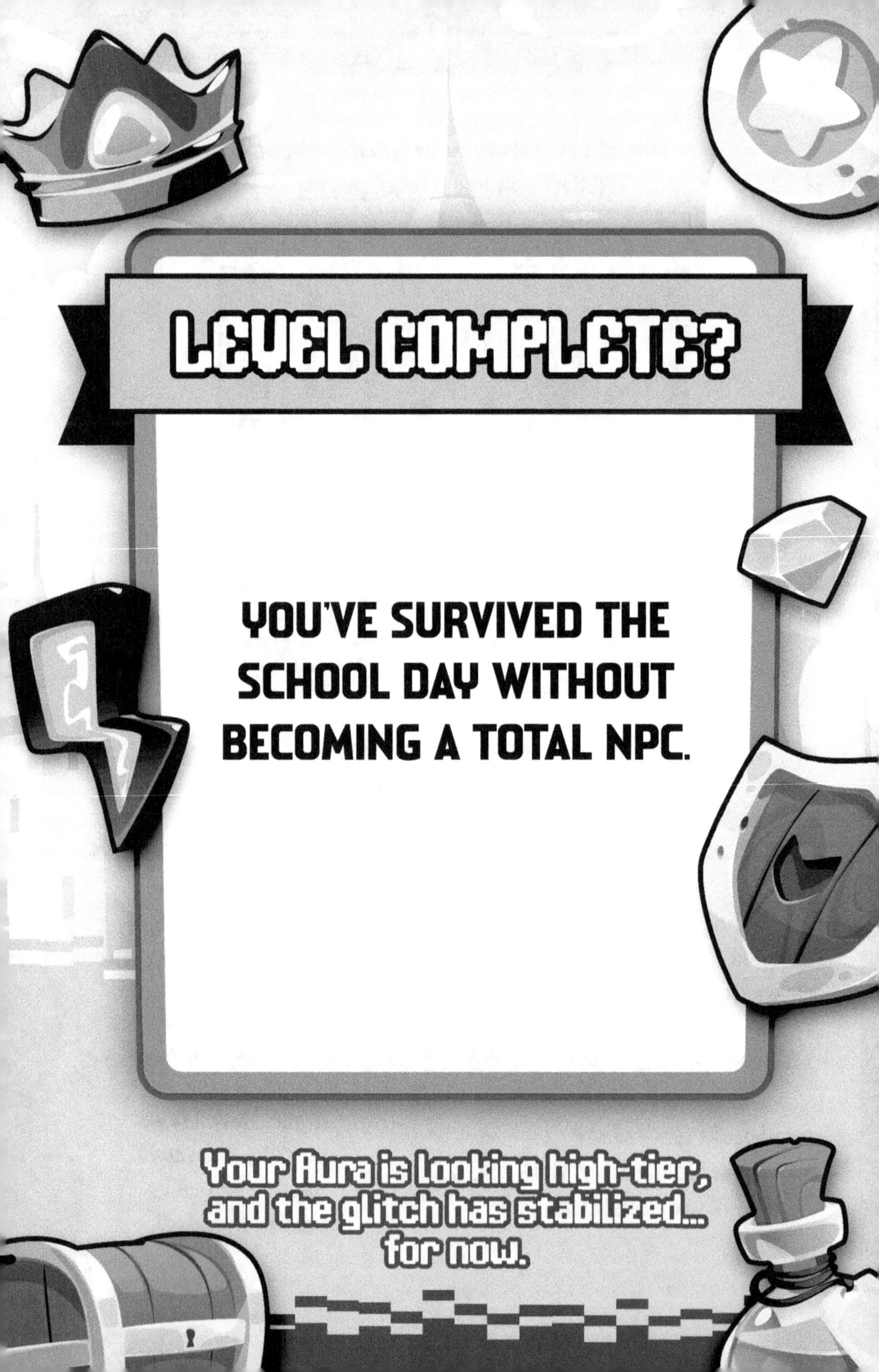
LEVEL COMPLETE?
YOU'VE SURVIVED THE SCHOOL DAY WITHOUT BECOMING A TOTAL NPC.
Your Aura is looking high-tier, and the glitch has stabilized... for now.

LEVEL 11
THE REALITY RIP

You've reached Floor 11, and the simulation is officially cooked. This isn't just a fragmented foyer; this is a total system crash. The physics have inverted, textures are peeling off the walls, and the floor is literally made of lava (don't worry, it tastes like strawberry jam).

To survive this floor, you must navigate "Impossible Glitch" choices. If you hesitate, your character model might dissolve into pure pixels.

THE "IMPOSSIBLE GLITCH" CHALLENGES

Would you rather have the "Floor is Lava" glitch actually happen every hour,

have the ceiling turn into a giant trampoline that bounces you 6 feet high?

Would you rather have your voice glitch into a foghorn every time you whisper,

wear "Lead Sneakers" that make a massive CRUNCH sound with every step?

Would you rather have your gravity flip upside down for hours,

turn into a "2D Sprite" and only be able to walk sideways like a platformer?

Would you rather have a Mini-Map of the world that is 7 years out of date,

a compass that only points toward the nearest snacks?

Would you rather
have it snow inside your house

OR have it rain purple
soda in your bedroom?

Would you rather
see the world entirely
in Minecraft blocks

see everyone
as a 2D Stick Figure?

Would you rather
have a giant "Error
Message" floating in
your field of vision

a "Loading" bar
on your chest that stays
stuck at 99%?

Would you rather every liquid you drink turn into edible glitter

every solid food you eat turn into bubbles?

Would you rather have a "Glitchy Pet" that swaps between a dog and a toaster,

a shadow that runs away to play pranks on you?

Would you rather have "Static Electricity" hair that shocks anyone within 6 inches,

skin that glows like a neon "Game Over" sign?

Would you rather hear different songs playing at once in your head,

have your nose play a loud "Taco Bell" bell sound every time you blink?

Would you rather have your "Character Model" be 6 times wider than normal,

be so thin you're basically invisible when you turn sideways?

Would you rather repeat the same 7 words for the rest of your life,

forget your own name but remember every meme ever made?

Would you rather have "No-Clip" mode turned on (walk through walls but risk falling through the map)

"Lag-Teleport" into a random room every 6 steps?

Would you rather your "Inventory" spill out of your pockets,

have your pockets be mini Black Holes that swallow your phone?

Would you rather have a cape that lets you fly (but only 6-7 inches off the ground)

"Speed Boots" that only work when you're underwater?

Would you rather have your face Pixelate whenever you're embarrassed,

have a giant floating "W" or "L" appear over your head based on your Aura?

Would you rather be followed by a "Glitchy Ghost" of your younger self

a "Future Version" of yourself who only speaks in riddles?

Would you rather all your furniture turn into giant gummy bears

your walls turn into touch-screens that only play "Brainrot" edits?

Would you rather speak only in Auto-Tune for a week,

only be able to communicate using emotes and victory dances?

Would you rather have a "Double Jump" that makes a loud "Boing" sound,

be able to breathe underwater, but it tastes like salty pickles?

Would you rather have your Drip change randomly every few minutes

be stuck in a "Hot Dog" suit that gives you +10,000 Aura?

Would you rather have your hands turn into random tools (spatulas/wrenches)

OR have your feet turn into wheels that never stop rolling?

Would you rather have a "Hitbox" that is way too big (you bump into everything),

be so small you can ride on the back of a squirrel?

Would you rather have a remote that can pause people for 7 seconds,

a remote that can change the color of the sky?

Would you rather have your "Save File" deleted

have to play life on "One-Hit-KO" mode (one trip and you reset the level)?

Would you rather have 7 extra lives but look like a generic NPC,

have one life but have the Aura of a 100-foot Titan?

Would you rather have your arms grow 6 feet long

have your neck stretch like a noodle whenever you're curious?

Would you rather have "Glitchy Luck" (find $100 then immediately trip in mud)

"Steady Luck" (nothing ever happens, you are a total NPC)?

Would you rather fix the Glitch and become the Hero,

stay in the chaos and become the 6-7 King of the Backrooms?

LEVEL COMPLETE?
YOU'VE SURVIVED THE REALITY RIP! THE SIMULATION IS HOLDING TOGETHER BY A SINGLE THREAD.
Your Aura is vibrating at a frequency that shouldn't be possible.

LEVEL 12

THE MEGA-FLEX ZONE

Welcome to The Mega-Flex Zone. You've reached the upper atmosphere of the Mega-Vault, where the air smells like "New Car" scent and the floors are made of solid gold (which is actually a major slipping hazard). This floor is all about Clout.

In this level, "luxury" is taken to a ridiculous scale. You'll have to choose between massive wealth and infinite fame, but watch out! If you flex too hard, you might just crash the simulation.

THE "MEGA-FLEX" CHALLENGES

Would you rather own a fleet of 7 private jets but have zero pilots,

own one paper airplane that actually flies you anywhere in the world?

Would you rather have 6 billion followers but absolutely no WiFi,

have 7 followers who e-transfer you $1,000 every time you post a mid meme?

Would you rather live in a house made of solid gold that is always slightly too hot,

a house made of ice where the thermostat is stuck on freezing?

Would you rather have a "7" Aura rating and be a billionaire,

have "Infinite Aura" but you have to live in a cardboard box (with 10G WiFi)?

Would you rather be followed everywhere by a full marching band playing your theme song

a personal paparazzi team that takes 7,000 photos of you a day?

Would you rather have a swimming pool filled with 6 million chocolate coins

a bathtub filled with real diamonds that are incredibly pointy and uncomfortable?

Would you rather have a lunchbox that dispenses gourmet 5-star meals

a backpack that spit-fires $100 bills every time you finish your homework?

Would you rather wear a crown that weighs 7 pounds and is encrusted with "glitchy" emeralds

a cape made of thousands of crisp, un-foldable dollar bills?

Would you rather be the "CEO of Aura Farming"

the "King of the Mega-Vault" with an army of robots to do your chores?

Would you rather
have a 7-star hotel in your backyard

OR a private island
that is shaped exactly like your own face?

Would you rather
have a pet dragon that
breathes multi-colored fire

a pet unicorn
that only eats gold-plated
carrots?

Would you rather
have every "Flex"
you do go viral,

be so rich you can buy your
school and turn it into a
multi-story arcade?

Would you rather have Infinite Clout, but you have to speak in a Victorian British accent forever,

be a total NPC but own 7 luxury yachts?

Would you rather drink a 24-karat gold smoothie

eat a pizza topped with edible glitter and diamonds?

Would you rather have a flying car that only moves at 7 mph,

a mountain bike that goes 200 mph but is made of heavy, solid gold?

Would you rather flex on your enemies by owning 6 space stations

by having a voice that sounds like a professional movie trailer narrator?

Would you rather have a bedroom that is 7 times bigger than your actual house,

a bed made of 7,000 literal fluffy clouds?

Would you rather have your name written in the stars by the constellations

have your face printed on every currency note in the world?

Would you rather be able to "Buy" any superpower you want for 7 minutes at a time,

have one weird, useless superpower for free forever?

Would you rather have a closet that automatically spawns the "Best Drip" in the world,

a fridge that is always stocked with 6-7 billion snacks?

Would you rather have a 7-ton statue of yourself in the city center

a 7-inch mini-me statue that follows you around and cheers for you?

Would you rather be famous for being the "Main Character" of a blockbuster movie

for being the person who finally "Broke the Simulation"?

Would you rather have a "Diamond Mewing Streak" that gives you +6,700 Aura,

a "Golden Voice" that makes everyone do what you say?

Would you rather own 6 robot butlers who are all clumsy NPCs,

one super-intelligent AI who thinks all your jokes are "Mid"?

Would you rather be the first person to reach 6.7 trillion Aura points

the first person to actually escape the Mega-Vault?

Would you rather have clout so high you get a 70% discount at every store,

be so rich you don't even look at the price tags?

Would you rather have sneakers made of rare space metals

a hoodie that stays perfectly clean even if you fall in a puddle of ketchup?

Would you rather
have your birthday party on a massive yacht

OR on a private moon base
with alien DJs?

Would you rather
have a "Flex" that is
"No Cap" (everyone
believes you),

a flex that is
"All Cap" but you still get
the clout anyway?

Would you rather
have 6-7 Billion Aura and
be the "Legend of the Vault"

trade it all in for
a "Secret Ending" that no
one else gets to see?

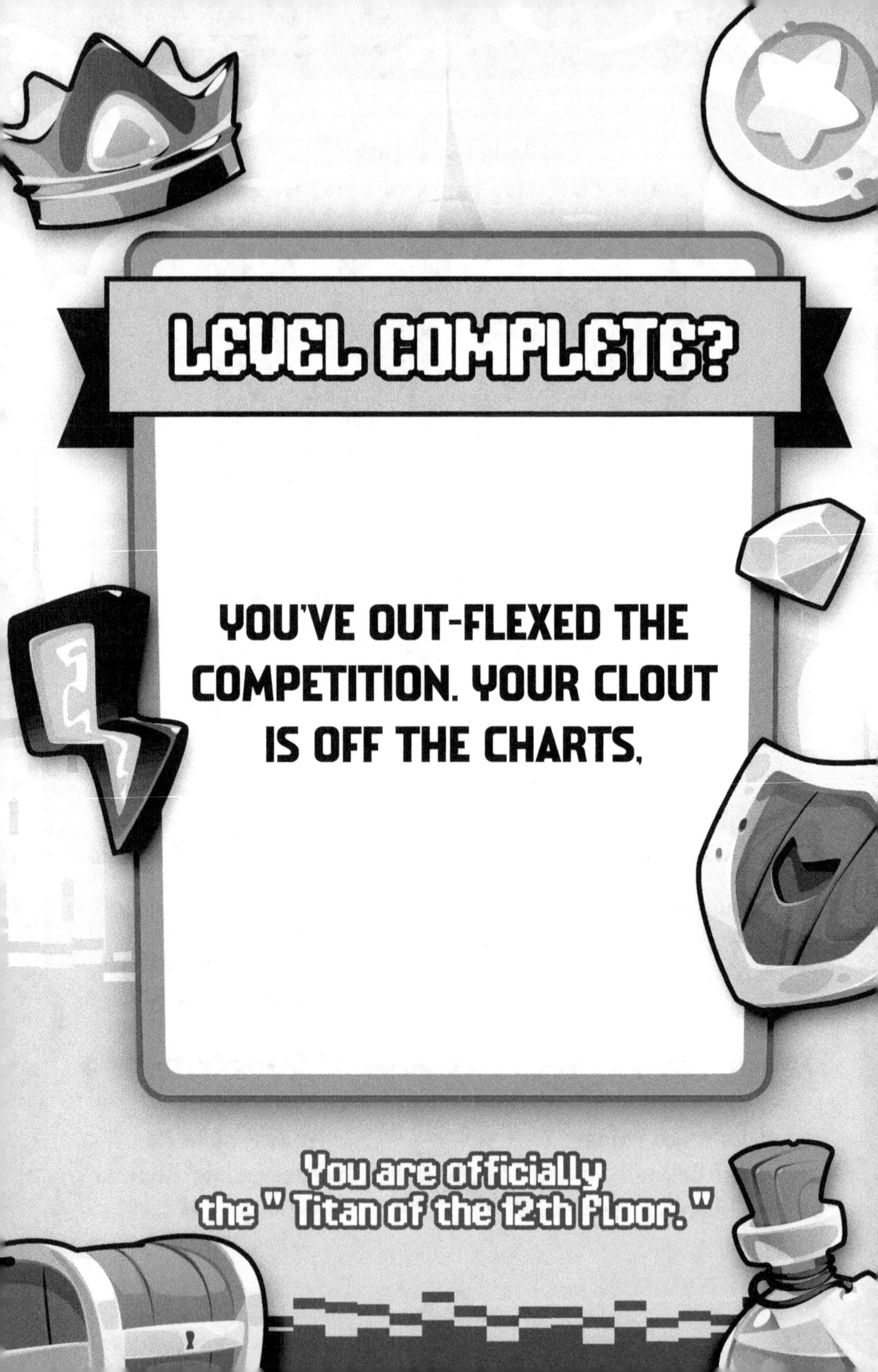
LEVEL COMPLETE?
YOU'VE OUT-FLEXED THE
COMPETITION. YOUR CLOUT
IS OFF THE CHARTS.
You are officially
the " Titan of the 12th Floor. "

LEVEL 13
THE 6-7 TIME WARP

You've reached the penultimate floor! The clock is literally breaking. On this level, the past, the future, and the most legendary memes are colliding into one giant "6-7" scale mess. One second you're dodging a T. rex, and the next you're explaining "Skibidi" to a Victorian ghost.

To clear this floor and reach the Omega Aura Overlord, you must navigate the timeline without losing your Aura to the "Cringe of the Past" or the "Chaos of the Future."

THE "RETRO & ROBOT" CHALLENGES

Would you rather ride a T. rex to school that eats your backpack every morning,

zip around the future on a hoverboard that never stops spinning?

Would you rather time-travel for 6 years with a robot that loses your snacks

with a pirate who insists on calling you "Captain Stinkyface"?

Would you rather wear a knight's armor that clanks every time you blink

a squeaky spacesuit that launches confetti every time you sneeze?

Would you rather get stuck in a medieval castle guarded by 700 chickens

in a futuristic lab run by over-caffeinated squirrels?

Would you rather attend
an 1800s school with a goat for a teacher,

OR a futuristic school where your desk floats away
if you stop paying attention?

Would you rather
speak only like a dramatic
Shakespearean actor

like a "glitchy" robot
that says "Beep-Boop"
every 6-7 seconds?

Would you rather
take a bath in a Roman tub
filled with 7 tons
of spaghetti

in a zero-gravity
bubble bath with
a singing robot duck?

Would you rather meet a caveman who thinks your phone is a snack,

your future self who has been "Floss Dancing" since 2017?

Would you rather be stuck in the Ice Age for 6 centuries with frozen cereal,

in the year 4000, where everything smells like cinnamon?

Would you rather ride a woolly mammoth through a grocery store

a time-traveling bicycle that hiccups every time you pedal?

Would you rather be best friends with a dragon who loves ancient memes

a robot cat that won't stop correcting your grammar?

Would you rather visit ancient Egypt and accidentally sneeze on a Pharaoh,

travel 7 centuries into the future and be mistaken for a talking sandwich?

Would you rather babysit a baby dinosaur who drools lava

a future alien toddler who thinks you're its pet for the next 6 years?

Would you rather build a spaceship with your great-great-grandkids

a sandcastle with a confused caveman who tries to eat the sand?

Would you rather get stuck in a time loop on the day you had 6 dozen cupcakes,

teleport to a random century every time you cough?

Would you rather be the world's most famous knight who's allergic to horses,

the first kid on Mars who is terrified of space suits?

Would you rather go to a 1970s disco in glow-in-the-dark bell-bottoms

a future rave with laser shoes that never turn off?

Would you rather take a math test in the year 1600 with a feather quill

in the year 4000 with a talking calculator that roasts your outfit?

Would you rather cook dinner with cavemen who only eat bugs,

at a future robot diner where every meal is a 7-layer purple cake?

Would you rather travel in a time machine made of skateboards

one held together by a million bubblegum bubbles?

Would you rather enter a future talent show with a robot octopus judge

a medieval joust where your horse is a giant bouncy castle?

Would you rather bring a dinosaur to your birthday party

bring a future alien to your dentist appointment for a checkup?

Would you rather write your name on the first cave wall in history,

OR have a statue of you in the year 5000 that looks incredibly cursed?

Would you rather go camping with a caveman who steals your marshmallows

a future explorer who thinks tents are actually hats?

Would you rather compete in the ancient Olympics wearing a toga,

the Mars Olympics, where the floor is a 7-ton trampoline?

Would you rather invent a skateboard made of solid rock

the first robot that only knows 7 different knock-knock jokes?

Would you rather time-travel by sneezing (zero control!)

by spinning in circles while shouting "Taco Tuesday!" for 6 minutes?

Would you rather live in a world where dinosaurs never went extinct,

one where flying cars get stuck in traffic for 6-7 hours?

Would you rather explain a smartphone to Benjamin Franklin

explain a tiny kazoo to a giant robot emperor?

Would you rather be the only kid in history with a time-traveling goat

the only one in the year 3000 who still uses a wooden pencil?

LEVEL COMPLETE?
THE TIMELINE IS RESTORED! YOU'VE SURVIVED THE WARP, AND YOUR AURA IS OFFICIALLY TIMELESS.
You are now standing at the very top of the Vault. The Omega Aura Overlord awaits.

LEVEL 14
THE OMEGA AURA OVERLORD

You've reached the summit of the Mega-Vault. The air is heavy, distorted by the sheer weight of your progress. Before you stands the Omega Aura Overlord, a towering glitch in the simulation composed of pure neon energy and "Final Boss" energy, to "Beat the Game" and ascend to Legend status, you must pass the final Aura Check.

There are no NPCs here. There is no "Mid" allowed. Every choice you make will either cement your status as a God-Tier Titan or crash your game back to the Foyer of Fragmentation.

THE FINAL AURA CHECK

Would you rather defeat the Titan Boss by Mewing for 7 hours straight

by winning a dance battle against a 60-foot-tall robot?

Would you rather have "Final Boss" theme music play every time you walk into a room,

have a glowing "W" follow you everywhere like a pet?

Would you rather have Infinite Aura but be completely invisible to everyone,

have Zero Aura but everyone treats you like the Main Character?

Would you rather be able to pause real life for 6 minutes whenever you want,

be able to "Fast Forward" through any cringe moment instantly?

Would you rather have a massive statue of yourself built at the entrance of the Mega-Vault,

have your name coded into the "Final Credits" of reality?

Would you rather own the 7 most legendary items in the simulation,

have the power to code your own custom world from scratch?

Would you rather live as a Titan in a world of NPCs

live as an NPC in a world where everyone else is a 60-foot Titan?

Would you rather unlock a "Secret Ending" where you become the new Boss of the Vault,

an "Epic Ending" where you escape with 7 Billion Aura points?

Would you rather wear the Ultimate Drip (a suit made of literal starlight)

have Ultimate Strength (the ability to bench-press a planet)?

Would you rather have a 7-star kitchen that spawns any food you crave instantly,

OR a 7-star wardrobe that updates itself with the best drip every morning?

Would you rather be the Main Character of the entire Internet for 7 years

the secret hero who saved the world from a Mega-Glitch without anyone knowing?

Would you rather have an Aura so powerful it makes electronics lag when you walk by,

have the power to "Un-Cringe" any situation with a snap of your fingers?

Would you rather be stuck in the "Final Boss" room with your 6 best friends forever,

escape alone to a world where you are the only person with Aura?

Would you rather have your final victory announced by a massive foghorn

have your name whispered by every person on Earth at the exact same time?

Would you rather be able to Double Jump in real life

be able to teleport to any party in the universe instantly?

Would you rather have a pet Titan that is 7 times bigger than your house,

a pocket-sized Titan that gives you +1,000 Aura every morning?

Would you rather own the Master Key that opens any door in history,

the Aura Shield that protects you from ever taking an "L" again?

Would you rather
have your life turned
into a 7K resolution
cinematic masterpiece

a retro 8-bit game
that never ends?

Would you rather
be "No Cap" (unable to lie)
for the rest of your life,

have everyone
believe every "Cap" you tell,
no matter how delusional?

Would you rather
stay in the Mega-Vault as
the Ultimate Omega Aura
Overlord

wake up in the real world
with a permanent
"Aura Glow" that
everyone can see?

Would you rather
have a "Life Rewind"
button that only works
on your most "cooked"
moments,

a "Hype Man" who appears
from thin air to celebrate
every "W" you get?

Would you rather
be the only person who
can see the "Simulation
Code" of the world,

be the only person
who can never be "Ratio'd"
on the Internet?

Would you rather have a voice that can command 7,000 dragons

a mind that can solve any "Impossible Glitch" in under 6 seconds?

Would you rather have the ability to "Clip" any moment of your life to show people later,

have a "Mini-Map" in your peripheral vision that shows you where the nearest "Vibes" are?

Would you rather always have a 100% Battery Charge on every device you touch,

have Super-Speed Wi-Fi follow you even in the middle of the desert?

Would you rather be a legendary gamer who wins every tournament but has zero followers,

a top-tier influencer who is secretly terrible at every game they play?

Would you rather be able to speak every human language fluently

be able to communicate with the AI that runs the simulation?

Would you rather
have a Flying Mount that looks like a neon dragon

OR a Hyper-Car that
can drive over water and never runs out of fuel?

Would you rather
have the power to delete
any "L" from your past
so everyone forgets it
happened,

have the power
to duplicate any "W"
so it happens twice?

Would you rather
have your life narrated
by a professional voice actor

have a health bar
floating over your head
that makes you invincible
until it hits zero?

GAME CLEAR!
YOU DEFEATED THE
OVERLORD.
YOUR FINAL SCORE: 6.7
TRILLION AURA POINTS. YOU'VE
NAVIGATED THE GLITCHES,
SURVIVED THE LAG, AND
OUT-FLEXED THE SIMULATION.
You are officially
NOT AN NPC.

THE EXIT PORTAL:

MISSION COMPLETE

SYSTEM STATUS: [STABLE] AURA LEVELS: [INFINITE] NPC STATUS: [REJECTED]

Congratulations, Titan.

You've done the impossible. You climbed 15 floors of pure, unadulterated chaos. You survived the 6-7 ton snacks, the reality-ripping glitches, and the most "Cringe" corridors the Mega-Vault could throw at you. You didn't just play the game; you ratioed it.

As you step through the final Exit Portal and return to reality, remember: Aura is permanent. You are no longer just a kid with a book; you are a Level 14 Legend. You have the Drip of a champion and the mindset of a Sigma.

THE TITAN'S FINAL DEBRIEF:

- **The 6-7 Rule:** You now know that when things get "heavy," you just get stronger.
- **No Cap:** You've learned to spot the glitches and choose the path with the most glory.
- **Main Character Energy:** You've proven that you aren't just following a script; you're writing it.

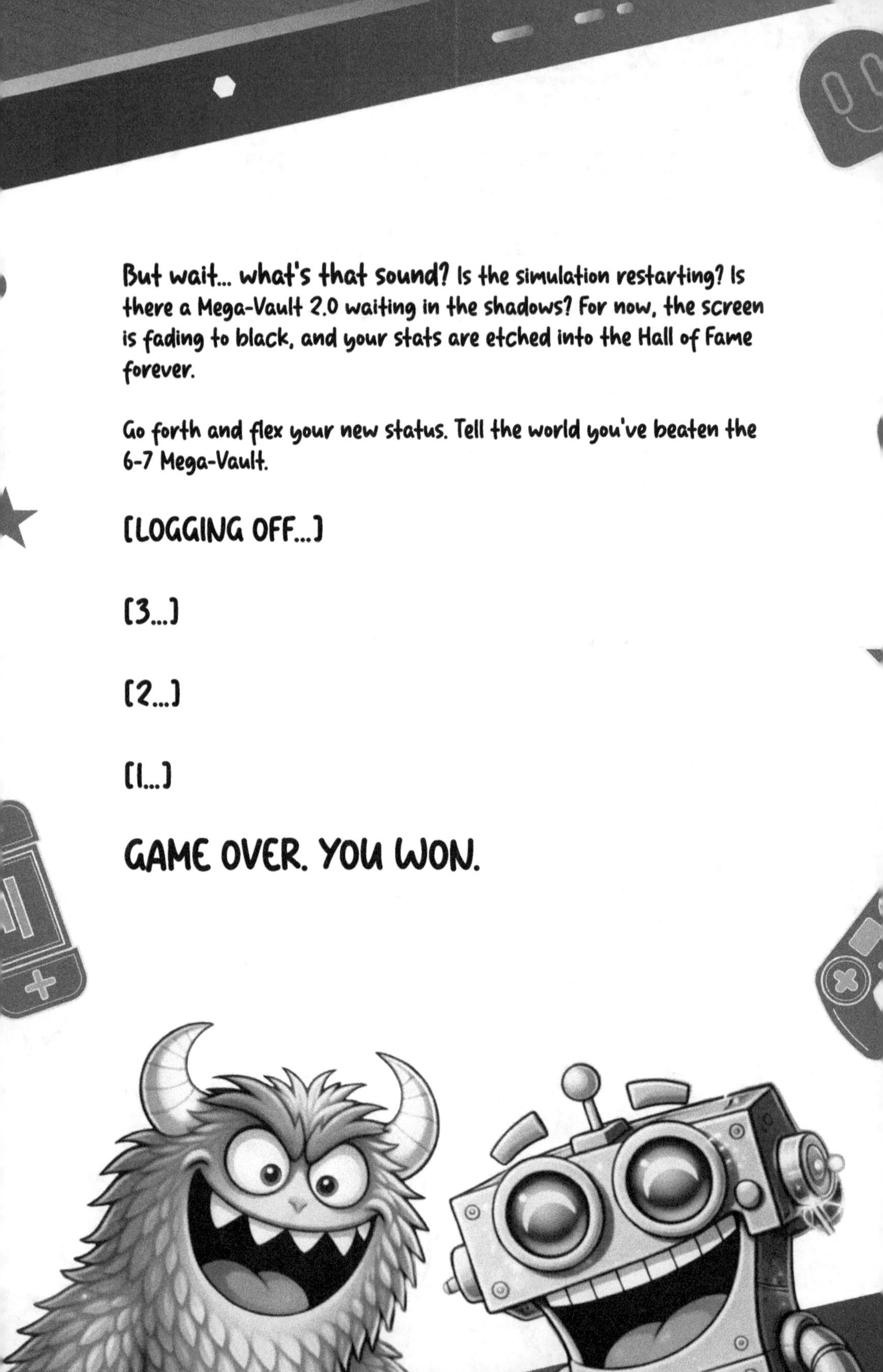

But wait... what's that sound? Is the simulation restarting? Is there a Mega-Vault 2.0 waiting in the shadows? For now, the screen is fading to black, and your stats are etched into the Hall of Fame forever.

Go forth and flex your new status. Tell the world you've beaten the 6-7 Mega-Vault.

[LOGGING OFF...]

[3...]

[2...]

[1...]

GAME OVER. YOU WON.

If you did, we are ecstatic. If not, please write your complaint to us, and we will ensure we fix it.

If you're feeling generous, there is something important that you can help me with... tell other people that you enjoyed the book.

Ask a grown-up to write about it on Amazon. When they do, more people will find out about the book. It also lets Amazon know that we are making kids around the world laugh. Even a few words and ratings would go a long way.

If you have any ideas or jokes that you think are super funny, please let us know. We would love to hear from you. Our email address is:

RIDDLELAND@RIDDLELANDFORKIDS.COM

ABOUT RIDDLELAND

Riddleland is a mum + dad-run publishing company. We are passionate about creating fun and innovative books to help children develop their reading skills and fall in love with reading. If you have suggestions for us or want to work with us, shoot us an email at

RIDDLELAND@RIDDLELANDFORKIDS.COM

Our family's favorite quote:

"Creativity is an area in which younger people have a tremendous advantage since they have an endearing habit of always questioning past wisdom and authority."

Bill Hewlett

www.ingramcontent.com/pod-product-compliance
Lightning Source LLC
Chambersburg PA
CBHW061528050726
47593CB00002B/717

* 9 7 8 1 9 5 7 5 1 5 5 5 7 *